To Scott

THE POEMS OF WING LEI

Sanders Grant

The Poems of Wing Lei

Alex Grant

Wind Publications

Copyright © 2012 by Alex Grant. Printed in the United States of America. All rights reserved. No part of this book may be reproduced in any manner, except for brief quotations embodied in critical articles or reviews. For information, address Wind Publications, 600 Overbrook Drive, Nicholasville, KY 40356.

International Standard Book Number 978-1-936138-45-6
Library of Congress Control Number 2012932494

First edition

Acknowledgments

Thanks to *Pirene's Fountain*, *Ithica Lit* and Jacar Press's *Love Anthology* for first publication of some of these poems ("The Bonsai Master," "Buddha Dream," "Song," "Hymn," "Wine," "On Waking from a Dream," and "The Hanging Temple at Hengshan").

I offer thanks to my wife and reader-in-chief, Tristi DeBlander, for her careful reading and her unstinting encouragement and optimism.

— For Tristi —

This book is dedicated to the spirit of Wing Lei —
and to the memory of Li Po, Wang Wei and Tu Fu .

"In order to overcome the tiger, you must become the serpent."

— Wing Lei

A monk-poet born in the JiangXi province of China in the mid-9th century, Wing Lei was a contemporary of the Chinese poetry masters Li Po, Tu Fu, and Wang Wei. His early life was spent in relative anonymity as a mid-level government official in the province, though it is known that he wrote poetry during this time. When his beloved wife Nagini was drowned in a flood during the spring of her thirty-fifth year, Wing Lei gave up his government position and took vows at a nearby monastery. He spent seven years there before embarking on his travels, writing poetry and living on the charity of those he met in the Chinese countryside. He is believed to have died in his sixty-first year. These poems are the story of his life and travels.

Contents

1

Buddha Dream	5
The Bonsai Master	6
Wine	7
At The Doll Shop	9
Hymn	10
Song	11
On Waking From a Dream	13
Dust	14

2

The Flea	21
Mountain Road	22
Storm	24
The Inn-Keeper's Wife	25
The Tea House	27
The Coming War	28
Twilight	30
The Priest	31

3

Dream	37
The Mad Woman	38
The Drowning	40
The Gardener	41
In the Sake-House	43
Waiting for the Ferry to Nanjing	44

4

The Calligrapher	51
Climbing T'ai Mountain	52
Leaves Falling from The Mulberry Tree	54
Morning, JiangXi Monastery, September 891	55
The Baker	57
The Hanging Temple at Hengshan	58
Nagini	60

About the Author	63

— 1 —

"Without stirring abroad, one can know the whole world; without looking out of the window, one can see the way of heaven. The further one goes, the less one knows."

— Lao Tzu

the poet wanders the countryside

Buddha Dream

Things you will hold today: a small cloud, a murder of cawing crows, the incoming rainstorm. Also the white evening, pulling at something you are almost unable to name.

Realize this may all be a dream — a figment of some imagination — but who's to say you won't wake tomorrow under the Bodhi tree — wheeling universe at your fingertips.

The Bonsai Master

Sculpts the landscape of the minuscule through a looking-glass —
trimming the boughs with a tiny saw wired to a pencil, stripping

the leaves with an ant glued to a nail board — precise as the white
peony petals unfolding like a heart under the surgeon's knife, red

pistils spattering eggs and pollen — brazen fluttering at the wind.

Wine

There are times when an afternoon seems to last a lifetime —
five hours in this drinking-den, and I have no wish to leave.

The best of my self is here, in the thin swishing of plum wine
in my cup — in the laughter of the serving-girl — who reminds

me of my daughter — in the ruddy faces of men who accept that
their youth is behind them, in the tapestry flapping like a shawl

above the door, the sun appearing and disappearing behind it —
like small moments of realization — floating to earth like petals.

The Buddha sat for forty-nine days under the Bodhi tree, waiting for enlightenment. Two hours under this Juniper and all I can think

of is Nagini. Thus is the second noble truth of the accumulation of suffering.

At The Doll Shop

The Genshai's wife holds the edge of her kimono above a puddle —
stoops under the lintel, her comb grazing the pine. Her man holds

a parasol above her shoulder, smiles and cocks his head at a pretty
girl passing by — she lowers her head and giggles, then turns to look

back at him. A scraggy chicken pecks in the dirt, her feathers slick
with rain. I can see the lady through the flapping screen — running

her fingers over the china-doll's face, looking like a young girl who
just unwrapped a birthday gift — I watch the chicken peck at a tick,

see it disappear into that ragged mouth — and now I see the lights
go on in the sake-house — I twist the coins in my pocket between

my fingers, cross the street, past the lady and her man, red package
under his arm — his hand resting on her waist like a firefly on a leaf.

Hymn

You berate the clouds for not being made of sterner stuff — harangue the trees for their constant bending to the wind — curse the vacuous infirmity of the sky, puddled with faint stars — wheeling night after night in their abject predictability.

I gave you celestial — you raised armies against the heavens. I taught you every secret language — you have only one word for lightning, hundreds for death.

And then I hear you sing — and forget again what it is that you want from me.

Song

The priest sweeps the walkway with a bristle broom — dust-motes floating like tiny clouds of sunlight. His robe — once stitched with gold — is tattered

now, flapping in the early evening breeze with the ragged red prayer-flags at the top of the hill. He is humming a song his father taught him — a song

of a man who walks through a forest in winter, shoeless, his shirt shredded by rose-thorns and brambles — his skin chapped by the thin wind. The man

smiles and breaks into a run — he sees the edge of the forest up ahead, hears the temple bell clanging — the night sky wheeling and fizzling like a cannon-

fuse as it melts into the ocean, hissing stars disappearing below the horizon, and now he is slowly melting into the earth — the bells fading like a passing

circus, stars blinking out above him, his wife's voice calling his name, waves washing over his eyes like pebbles on a shore-line, priests of stone and dust.

Thunder and lightning on the mountain — the Gods grinding out the night.

On Waking From a Dream

In the middle of the night, I wake and sit upright,
see the moon hanging like a peach in a black tree.

I push myself up from the straw bed, stretch out
my arms and shuffle towards the light. My wife's

kimono — blue as an empty sky — flaps on the door,
wafts the faint scent of jasmine through the room.

I open the paper screen, step onto pine-needles,
smell the river and the mountain cherry-blossom.

I see her there, her head thrown back — laughing
at some story — she looks at me, holds her hands

up and waves, dives in slow-motion into the river.

Dust

Spiders small as specks of dust build their webs in the wash-bowl —
what do they hope to catch — could anything be so small that our

eyes cannot see? On that day when you become tinier than dust —
when the world shrinks from your eyes like the ebbing ocean tide,

when you become the all-consuming, enormous twilight — you will
think of the spider, of his tiny hanging web, oblivious and hopeful.

This song, so late in the evening — this bird, holding on to the day, singing his heart out.

— 2 —

"Heaven is high, Earth wide. Bitter between them flies my sorrow."

— *Li Po*

the poet by a waterfall

The Flea

Cares nothing for the world — not for the priest or the courtesan
or the peasant carrying bundles of gathered wood to the charcoal

ovens — not the young girl, wet from her morning swim, combing
her black hair by the river, not the wine-merchant plying the sake-

house owner with sweet compliments and bowls of yellow plums,
not the ragged dogs, not the soldiers stumbling from the garrison,

not the old poet brushing the straw from his hair — wondering why
the flea — faithless, indifferent — needs the flavor of so many bodies.

Mountain Road

Thunder off in the distance — cherry-blossom scent surrounds me. My knapsack is heavy with ripe licorice and wolfberries — bleeding

orange and black on my shirt. I think of the mountain hornet, his hairy knees and back, flying through raindrops the size of houses,

seeing the world through those eyes — yellow sting trailing behind.

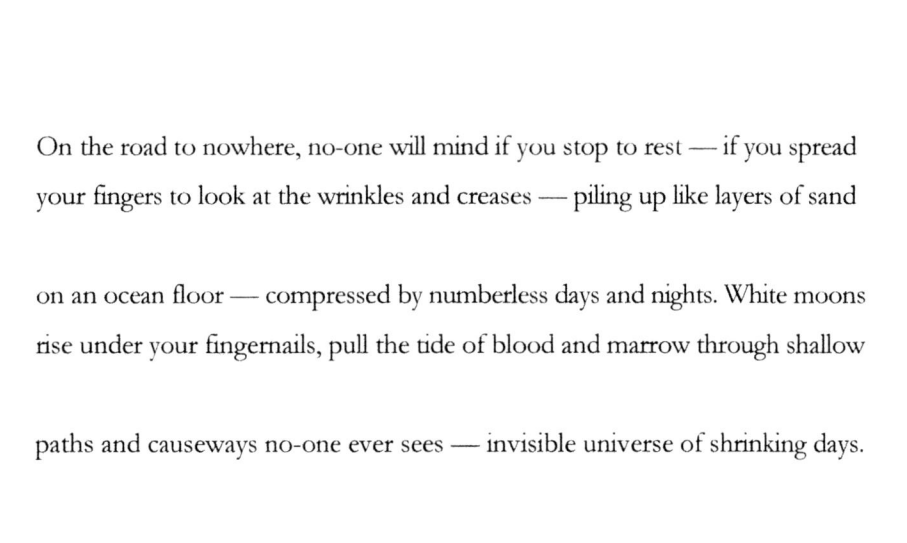

On the road to nowhere, no-one will mind if you stop to rest — if you spread your fingers to look at the wrinkles and creases — piling up like layers of sand

on an ocean floor — compressed by numberless days and nights. White moons rise under your fingernails, pull the tide of blood and marrow through shallow

paths and causeways no-one ever sees — invisible universe of shrinking days.

Storm

Lavender-pink sky over the mountain — the storm moves in

like a plug of lead dropped into a river. The smell of coming

rain blows in on the wind — the shop-window shutters clatter

as the lights go out one by one — a woman carrying a length

of red silk hurries past me, her bandaged feet scuffing clouds

of red dust up behind her — like a conquering army coming in

from the east, howling their promises in bright new languages.

The Inn-Keeper's Wife

Seven winters widowed, she shuffles through the market
in her black kimono — her eyes never leaving the ground.

Once, she was a story-teller, served plum wine and tea-eggs
to merchants from Nanjing — laughed at their playful jokes,

listened patiently to the stories of their wives and families,
led them to their straw beds when the wine or their thirsts

were dry — now the inn is quiet and shuttered, and she pours
the wine into a single cup and offers prayers to her husband.

I bow as she passes — she stops for a moment, looks at me
sideways. Without speaking, we exchange our condolences.

At the funeral, I drink Chrysanthemum wine in the garden. The widow washes her hands in the fountain, dabs her fingers to her lips — sighs and smiles faintly.

The world is an endless wedding, the guests dressing and undressing in the dark.

The Tea House

I push off my sandals, cross the threshold and bow toward the Buddha
on the far wall — a girl in a purple kimono leads me to a polished wood

table. A sprig of cherry blossom lies in the center of a plain white plate,
two sliced red plums arranged around it — the chopsticks rest on a white

napkin, pristine and perfectly square — the teapot and bowls, decorated
with pale yellow flowers, sit, centered, on a maple tray. The girl moves

to take a bowl away and I hold out my hand to cover it — she pours two
cups, bows, clasps her hands and backs away from the table — I pull out

the blue scarf from my pocket, hold it in my lap — then press it against
my face, inhale, catch the faint scent of sandalwood. Such attachments,

The Buddha would say, blind us to the truth of the universe — floating
through the world, we hold on like drowning men to driftwood, never

glimpsing our true natures — but tonight I will hold this small fragment
of silk, remembering too that the way is not in the sky — it is in the heart.

The Coming War

Through centuries, it seems, nothing has changed — the faint of heart,
the blameless — the well-meaning and confused — still caught between

the enemies and their enemies — between the despots and the heroes,
in a shadow-puppet play even children understand. In times of great

upheaval, the poet turns to the moon and wine and women, when all
things reveal themselves once again to be inches deep, universes wide.

I dreamed I was on a boat, far out in the ocean — the stars just above my head. My mother was pulling fish from the water, stroking and cooing each of them —

galaxies fell left and right — fizzling like small suns in a koi-pond. I grew smaller as the sun rose, fell through a crack between the boards — breathed in an ocean.

Twilight

Pulled by six golden dragons, Hsi Ho drives the sun-chariot
into the western sky — where the star river descends to earth,

touches the mountains, falls into the Yangtze — where poets,
following the sage in the cup, row out to catch the reflection

of the moon in the water, unmade music ringing in their ears
like half-remembered songs hummed by children in the night.

The Priest

Sits on the temple steps, spinning his prayer-wheel, his novitiate plucking tunelessly on the Ch'in — he chants under his breath, keeping perfect time

with the wheel's slow wobble. I mouth the prayers in time with him — *Lord Buddha, lift the veil from my eyes — let me leave the Wheel of Karma, spinning quietly*

under all creation, let me walk in the light of self-knowledge. Seven years in orders, and this truth never touched me as it does today — I clasp my hands, touch

my forehead and bow to the temple steps, my last prayer floating like a lily.

I sit under a willow, listening to the river — swilling wine I don't need in a cup.
A spider works at her web like a woman plucking a harp — waiting for the flies

and the moths who flutter mindlessly toward the moon to fill her empty belly.

— 3 —

Rain on a tin roof — apologetic tears of The Gods.

— Wing Lei

the poet listens to wind in the trees

Dream

I dreamed I saw the Sun-crows sitting in the mulberry tree, on the bitterest day of the year. They had something to tell me — but the wind blew hard, drowning

out everything but the sound of the river and the wine-flask clinking in my bag.

The Mad Woman

Her nails curl into her palms as she hunches up and offers to tell
my fortune — but first, she must tell me her story, how once, men

desired her, how they talked of her beauty in villages days distant,
how a prince once offered his kingdom for one night in her bed

how her suitors would stumble through rose-thorns and briars to
knock on her window — make love-songs no-one else ever heard.

The sky is on fire — thin clouds lit from below, blotches of indigo
between — she says this is her doing - that she controls the clouds,

the rain and the sun, that she knows how I grieve for Nagini, that
a hundred years from now, none of this will matter, and someone
else will sit on this rock and look at the sky and dream of the dead.

These are the notes no-one ever plays, the high and low registers out on the boundaries — the depths and heights beyond the blank landscape of the everyday — crucible of flowers and black clouds.

Lightning in the forest, rain on the ocean, the wind whipping waves into black walls no-one ever sees — the secrets of the world revealed to no-one in particular. Now wash your hands and brush your teeth —

and tomorrow, the jig-saw moments of the day will fit like coastlines.

The Drowning

His body floats like a bloated sack of rice torn by water-rats — shredded
jute hanging from his black and blue arms, belly poking out of the water.

He is a young man — no more than twenty — yesterday, he laughed with
his friend, teased the girl at the market stall, drank a flask of plum wine

in a single gulp — slammed it on the table and called for more. His father
once beat a man, close to death, for a gambling debt — spared him when

he promised to lay down the dice — now, knuckles bloodied by the rocks,
he pulls the boy from the water, calls out to The Buddha for forgiveness.

The Gardener

Moves from tree to tree like a bee on cherry-blossom — his fingers brushing
the blooms like a player plucking Ch'in-strings — he stoops, inhales the scent

of white Chrysanthemum, nods and bows his head to the orchestra of petals,
shoots and fronds — oblivious to everything but the quiet turning of the earth.

Today, I am immortal — I walk through the graveyard, humming a childhood song — grasshoppers jump at my feet, trilling short songs of summer and quiet acceptance.

The woodsman, whistling, hones his axe under the shade of the Cherry-blossom.

In the Sake-House

We all crave heaven, look for it in the wind blowing barley, the bird trilling, in the faces of those we meet. The direction of a room is enough to bring

it closer — the slant of the sun late in the day brings you back to the house of your grandmother — her pale ankles turning orange as she tells you that

on the day of your death, you must face west, give thanks — and remember.

Waiting for the Ferry to Nanjing

I can see the boatman on the opposite bank — a man after my own heart, he looks from side to side, reaches into the boat — and now he's tippling

from a wine-flask — he rubs his mouth with the back of his hand, throws the flask back and hoists his spindly legs over the gunwale. The flickering

light from his lantern makes a yellow snake in the water, a gibbous moon comes up over the mountain, turns the shore-line white, and I remember

waiting on this shore years ago after a thunderstorm — thinking about how I would soon be married, wondering how my life would change — throwing

the glob of opium into the lake — hearing it splash like a kingfisher diving.

Last night, the mountain burned — the tree-tops bending like wind-blown grass, smoke rolling in like fog on the ocean — I held a wet cloth to my face, watched

flames turn the earth black — knelt neck-high in the river — swallowed red water.

— 4 —

These shadow-puppet players —- waiting to meet the author.

— Wing Lei

the poet with student

The Calligrapher

He dips the brush into the inkwell — flicks the excess onto his leg and begins
to work on the parchment scroll — the pressure and tension of each character

precise and painstaking, the direction and thickness of each stroke capturing
the approximate in this exactitude of hand and eye and brush — a musician's

touch picking out each lingering note — each testament etched on white paper.

Climbing T'ai Mountain

On the ninth day of the ninth month, I celebrate my birth day by climbing to the top of T'ai Mountain to drink chrysanthemum wine. My grandfather

climbed Heaven's Gate in his seventieth year — left younger men huffing in the foothills, drained his wine-flask in a single gulp, called on the Gods

to bring him more — defiant to the end — daring Heaven to call him home.

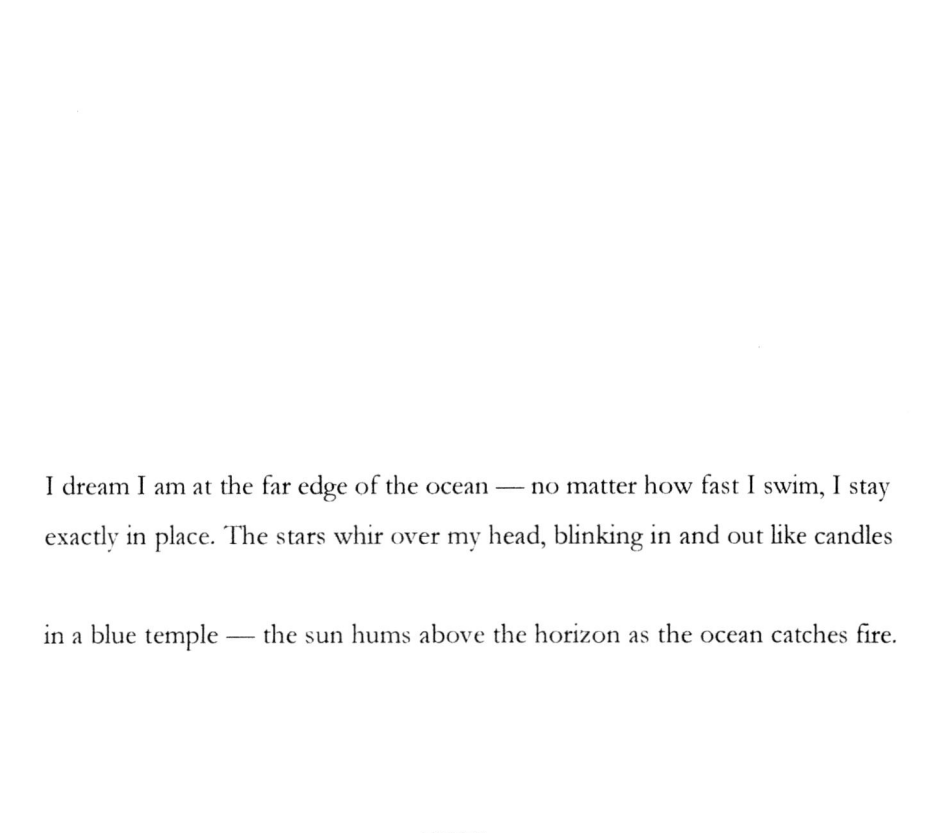

I dream I am at the far edge of the ocean — no matter how fast I swim, I stay exactly in place. The stars whir over my head, blinking in and out like candles

in a blue temple — the sun hums above the horizon as the ocean catches fire.

Leaves Falling from The Mulberry Tree

The Buddha said that all things must pass — sixty years, and finally I hear his words with a grain of understanding, this quiet acceptance brimming

up like a slowly breaking wave — I forgive all of it — the general marching his army toward nameless cities — the merchant who profits from the toil

of the poor, the drunken priest in the mountain temple — the poet selling his words for a bowl of rice, the woman making worthless potions from

licorice and opium — her customers always finding their way back to her — the beggars who robbed me while I slept — all fading like the sun setting

over T'ai Mountain — and I remember climbing into my grandmother's mulberry tree, my hands stained purple by the fruit, looking down onto

the garden below — wondering why she bowed to every flower and bush. Today my hands are blue as heaven. She looks up and beckons me down.

Morning, JiangXi Monastery, Autumn 891

The sun has not yet risen — I put the candle on the ledge above the wash-bowl, drench my face in cold water, savor the shock of still being in the world, while

wishing it were not so. I try too late to stifle the thought. Momentarily penitent, I ask Lord Buddha for forgiveness — turn my thoughts towards the coming day.

My life is in this cell — a bundle of clothes, scrolls of The Tao — an ink drawing of Nagini made by a young man whose smile I still remember — I bow towards

the rising sun, offer a prayer of thanks for the day — hear the temple bell clang.

I dreamed I stood on a plateau above a great plain — the river was ten thousand feet below — though I knew I could reach down and touch it — the wind burned my face,

the sun-crows cawed, a wave rose up like a mountain from the ocean above my head.

The Baker

He works the dough like a man squeezing a woman's shoulders,
hope and purpose squeezed and folded into shape — he flattens

the bing between his palms — throws it onto the iron pan — smiles
when the palm-oil sputters, the dough swelling like a frog's throat.

He is young, and sees my envy — he smiles and meets my eye — we
climb and descend the mountain — passing each other on the way.

The Hanging Temple at Hengshan

I climb through Mountain Ash and Rowanberry trees,
reach the promontory — see the foothills spread below.

The mountain goats of Tiger-Leaping Gorge, clattering
up the scree, stop to turn, rear up and butt heads — send

their bony echos clear across the valley. I drop my knap-
sack on wet pine-needles — pull out a flask of plum wine,

find a tea egg wrapped in rice-paper — mutter a small prayer
to Buddha. The wind changes direction — I hear prayer-bells

clang, inhale the scent of burning sandalwood — feel the blast
of the trumpets bounce inside my ears, the wine warming my

stomach. The monks chant the five remembrances — *I am sure
to become old, I am sure to become ill, I am sure to die, I am sure*

*to become separated from all that is dear to me, I am the owner
and heir of my actions* .... I pour another cup of wine and think

of my wife, of the boyhood games in my village, of the way
my grandmother's hands shook when she touched my hair —

I gulp the wine, watch a pair of red eagles riding the updrafts.

I dreamed I was washed onto the shore where the Sun-crows wait — smaller than a grain of rice, I shrank into the sand. They talked in a language I could not understand — wings

flapping like purple flags above a temple — and I was drowning by the shore, calling out to these birds who heard nothing — their blue beating wings washing me back out to sea.

Nagini

The poet Wing Lei wandered for years in search of his destiny, living on the kindness of others, on barley husks rubbed between his palms,

on laughter drifting from sake-huts on mountain roads. Years later, facing the universe on his straw bed, he recalled the girl in the pink kimono, who

smiled as she stepped from the ferry — Nagini — my heart stopped for you.

In loving memory of George Paton and Mary Arthur

Alex Grant has been a shepherd, a dental technician, a rope-maker, an electro-plater, an optical technician, a software applications developer and a Business Solutions Architect.
His poems have appeared in many notable U.S. national publications, he has released five poetry collections, and has received The Pavel Srut Poetry Fellowship, The Kakalak Poetry Prize, The Randall Jarrell Chapbook Prize and The Oscar Arnold Young Award(Best collection by a NC poet). He was one of 50 poets included in Best New Poets 2007, selected by Natasha Trethewey, the U.S. Poet Laureate. A 7-time Pushcart Prize nominee, he lives in Dumfries and Galloway with his wife Tristi, his dangling participles and his Celtic love of excess.

And now, the night sky -
Its infinite collection
Of luminous blue triangles.